LITTLE RED BAT

By Carole Gerber

Illustrated By Christina Wald

W9-ARK-230

A tiny foot clings to the stem of a leaf. The foot belongs to a little red bat. The bat, too, looks like a leaf.

It's a bright fall day, and a chilly wind whips through the forest. It shakes the leaves, blowing many to the ground.

The little bat shivers.

"Should I stay?" she wonders. "Or should I go?"

A moment later, the plump little bat lies on the ground. The leaf she clung to is beside her, blown down by the wind. Instantly, the little red bat curls herself into a ball and wraps her tail around her body. Now, the little red bat looks like a furry pine cone.

"Good trick," says a squirrel, burying nuts nearby.

The little red bat doesn't answer. She's shy and used to being alone. She seldom leaves her tree except at dusk, when she flies around eating insects. Lately, the little red bat has been eating more insects than usual.

"I said, 'good trick,'" repeats the squirrel.

The little red bat is pretty sure the squirrel only eats nuts. She uncurls her tail. "Thanks," she says.

"What are you doing here?" asks the squirrel as he digs. "Aren't you supposed to hang out in a cave?"

"I'm a tree bat," replies the little red bat. "I hang out in trees."

"How about that," the squirrel exclaims. "I'm a tree squirrel. My nest is up there!"

"Where will you live this winter?" asks the little red bat. "I'm wondering if I should stay or if I should go."

With a swish of his tail, the squirrel buries his last nut. "I'm staying. My winter food is all stored," he says. "If you stay, watch out for owls."

The little red bat watches the squirrel run up a tree. If she stays, will the leaves keep her warm? If she goes, which way should she fly?

The little red bat hears noises. Something is coming! Again, she rolls into a ball.

A deer stops to eat twigs. She's pretty sure deer don't eat bats. Still, the little red bat uncurls and creeps under a leaf pile.

The deer hears the leaves rustle. "Who's there?" he asks, ready to run.

"Just a bat trying to stay warm," the little red bat replies.

"Why are you still here?" asks the deer.

"Why are *you* still here?" asks the bat.

"I'm staying. The trees give me shelter, and I eat their twigs and bark," explains the deer. "What about you?"

"I can wrap up in my tail and stay here in the leaf pile," says the little red bat. "Or I can fly to a warmer place."

"If you stay, watch out for raccoons," warns the deer before trotting away.

The little red bat looks around. If a raccoon sees her, will it think she's a pine cone?

Behind her, the little red bat hears a crunching sound. In a panic, she stretches her wings.

"No need to fly off," says a rabbit that has been nibbling moss from the side of a tree. "I don't eat bats."

The little red bat knows this is true. From her leafy roost, she has seen rabbits eating moss, leaves, and little green things that pop up in spring.

"Are you staying or going?" asks the little red bat.

"Staying," says the rabbit.

"Will you sleep through the winter?" asks the little red bat.

"No," says the rabbit as she hops away. "I'll be out looking for food. If you stay, watch out for opossums."

The little red bat looks around. So many dangers! What should she do?

A chipmunk runs past, his cheeks filled with seeds. Moments later, he pops out of his burrow and looks at the little red bat with bright eyes.

"Stocking up for winter?" asks the little red bat.

"Yep," says the chipmunk as he scampers off to gather more food. "I sleep through most of it, but I wake up every once in a while to snack. If you can't hide in a burrow, watch out for hawks."

"Good-bye!" calls the little red bat, feeling as uncertain as ever. She searches the sky for hawks.

"Hey!" says a squeaky voice behind her.
The little red bat jumps, knocking over a tiny field mouse.
"Calm down!" snaps the field mouse. "I'm just passing through."
"Sorry! Are you heading south for the winter?" asks the little red bat.

"No, I was here eating tree roots," the field mouse explains. "Now I'm going back to my field to work on my tunnels."

"Then will you sleep through the winter?"

"No," says the field mouse as she scurries away. "I'll either be working or out looking for food. If you're outside this winter, watch out for foxes."

The little red bat sees a flash of color through the trees. Her heart flutters with fear. Is it a fox?

The little red bat relaxes. She's seen wild turkeys before. They're big, but they don't eat bats. This one is eating acorns.

"Filling up for winter?" asks the little red bat.

The turkey looks down at her with its small, dark eyes. "Yes," he says. "It looks like you've fattened up, too."

"I have," agrees the little bat. "Will you fly south or stay?"

"I'll roost in my tree at night and eat whatever I can find here in the daytime," explains the turkey. "Not bats!" he adds, as the little red bat backs away. "I eat mostly nuts and seeds."

"I eat mostly moths and mosquitoes," says the little red bat. "But there aren't any now. Since I've fattened up, I can sleep through winter or I can fly south."

"It's good you have a choice," replies the turkey as he rustles off through the leaves. "But if you stay, watch out for humans."

The little red bat again wonders what to do. She hears a scratching noise. So much goes on down here!

She watches a sparrow search for seeds among the weeds. The little red bat is not afraid of a bird that eats seeds.

"Hello," she says.

The sparrow looks surprised. "Why are you still here?" he asks.

"I'm wondering if I should stay or if I should go," replies the little red bat. Why are *you* still here?"

"I'm heading south with my flock this evening," says the sparrow, looking around. "Where's your flock?"

"I live alone in that tree," says the little red bat. "At least I used to."

"If you don't have a flock to follow, how will you know where to go?" asks the sparrow.

"I don't," the little red bat confesses.

The little bat watches as the sparrow scratches and pecks, scratches and pecks, filling up on seeds for his journey. When he has eaten his fill, the sparrow turns to the little red bat.

"If you stay, watch out for cats," he warns. "My flock will pass over soon after sunset. You're welcome to follow us."

The little red bat thinks about what she learned from the squirrel, the deer, the rabbit, the chipmunk, the field mouse, the turkey, and the sparrow. Each is prepared in its own way to survive winter.

She shudders as she recalls their warnings about owls, raccoons, opossums, hawks, foxes, humans, and cats.

Her mind is made up. The little red bat hops from the leaf pile and flies into her tree. She chooses a sturdy-looking leaf to cling to, tucks her wings, and falls asleep.

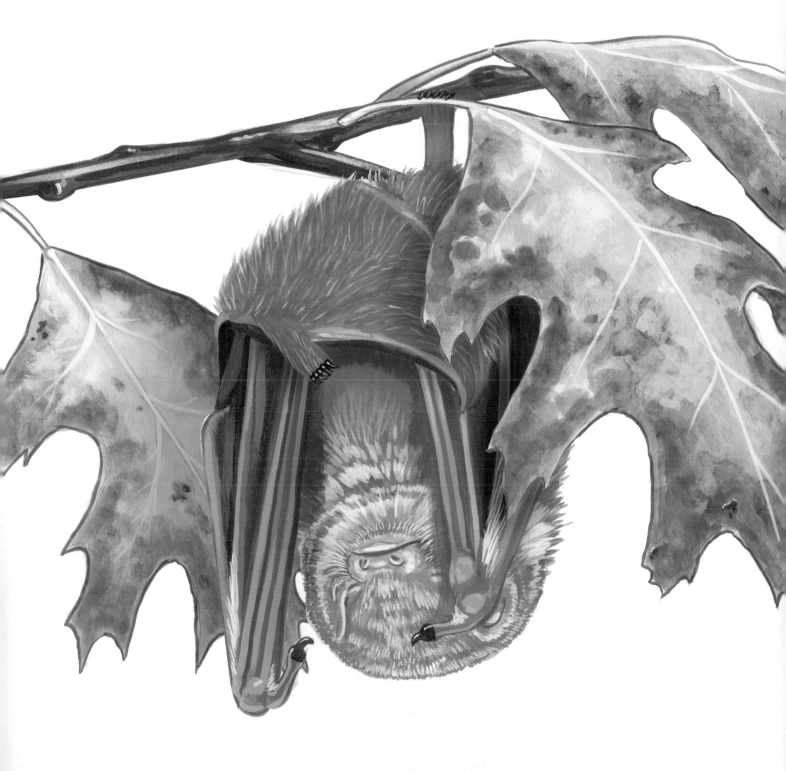

At dusk, the little red bat wakes and scans the sky. Sure enough, there's a flock of birds coming her way. When they fly over her tree, the little red bat lets go of the leaf and falls into flight.

For Creative Minds

The For Creative Minds educational section may be photocopied or printed from our website by the owner of this book for educational, non-commercial uses. Cross-curricular teaching activities, interactive quizzes, and more are available online. Go to www.SylvanDellPublishing.com and click on the book's cover to find all the links.

Match the Bat Adaptations

Match the bat's adaptations to the letters on the picture. Answers are upside down on the bottom of the page.

1 Bats' wings are their "hands." Each wing has five digit (finger) bones, just like our hands. Bats belong to the order, *Chiroptera*, a Latin word that means "hand-wing."

2 Bats use their large ears during echolocation. They make clicking noises with their mouth or nose, then listen for the echoes to bounce back. This lets them know where things are.

3 Long toes with sharp claws make it possible for bats to hang upside down from their roosts (where they sleep).

4 The saying "blind as a bat" is not true! Bats have very good light vision but use echolocation in the dark because it is easier than carrying a flashlight!

5 The bat's "thumb" has a claw at the end for climbing and holding food.

A

Bats can get rabies just like any mammal, but it's rare. Never touch any animal you do not personally know.

Some bats eat fruit and seeds. Bananas, cashews, and saguaro cactus are some of the plants that rely on bats for seed dispersal or pollination.

Most bats (including red bats) eat insects. A single little brown bat (*Myotis lucifugus*) can eat 600 mosquitoes in an hour!

Except for the polar regions and isolated islands, bats live all over the world.

Bats are not birds—they are mammals like us. They are warm-blooded, have fur, give birth to live babies, and produce milk to feed them. Bats are the only mammals that fly.

Answers: 1D, 2C, 3E, 4B, 5A

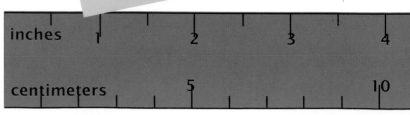

There are two types of red bats: Eastern Red Bats (*Lasiurus borealis*) and Western Red Bats (*Lasiurus blossevillii*).

Red bats are solitary creatures. Except for females raising their young, these bats live alone.

Red bats are among the fastest flying bats. Their speed has been measured at over 40 miles (64 km) an hour. They have such a distinctive way of dipping and diving as they fly that naturalists can identify them from far away.

5

D

1

3

4

2

B

C

E

There are over 1,000 types of bats. Red bats are one of the most common bats in North America.

Red bats roost in trees and their color helps them blend with their surroundings (camouflage). Other types of bats may roost in caves.

Bats hang upside down to rest and sleep. When they want to fly, they simply let go.

6   7   8   9   10   11   12   13

Red bats are tiny! They grow to be 4 or 5" (10-12 cm) with a 13" (33 cm) wingspan.

15   20   25   30

How Animals Deal with Seasonal Changes

Animals survive cold-weather winter in one of three ways: they adapt, migrate, or hibernate. How will each of the animals in the book spend their winter?

ADAPT: Animals either store food, as squirrels do, or eat the less tasty food that's available in winter and grow thicker coats that help them stay warm.

MIGRATE: Animals travel to a warmer place where their usual food supply is available. They return each spring when the earth warms and there is once again plenty to eat.

HIBERNATE: Animals stay put, their body temperature drops, and their breathing slows. The fat they have stored in their body keeps them alive through the winter.

Animals are not to scale.

Red Bats and Seasonal Changes

Red bats may migrate, hibernate, or do both. Some fly south and remain active through the winter. Red bats have been seen traveling in migratory waves along with small birds.

Bats are one of the few species that are "true hibernators." Once they conk out for the winter, they rouse themselves only occasionally to "answer calls of nature" (potty time!), to get a drink of water, and to snack lightly if they can find insects nearby. Some red bats, even in relatively cold climates, stay put. They wrap up in their furry tails and hibernate under leaf piles, fallen logs, or in hollow trees.

Bat Life Cycle Sequencing Activity

Put the red bat life-cycle events in order to spell the scrambled word.

A	Pups learn to fly when they are only three or four weeks old.
B	Pups cling to their mothers. When the mother leaves to hunt at night, she may carry a pup or it may hang from a small tree branch while she is gone.
D	Most bat pups are born naked or with minor peach fuzz.
E	Most bats give birth to only one pup per year, but red bats can have as many as four.
R	Female red bats become pregnant in the spring. The mother bat is pregnant for approximately three months.
T	Pups are weaned when they are five or six weeks old at which point they leave their mother.

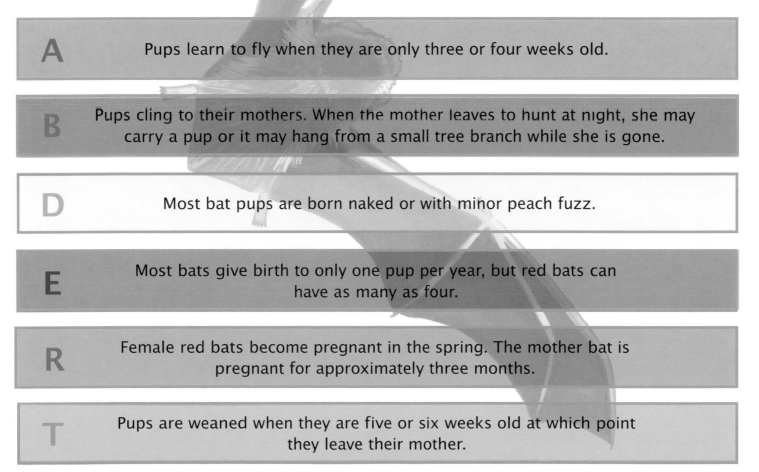

Answer: REDBAT

To Tyler Stephen DeLacey with love from Mimi

To Robert and Ann Walton, who opened their home to me to observe the red bat family they rescued and later released back into the wild. It was invaluable to observe these fascinating little bats up close which immennsely improved my ability to illustrate them. Thank you also to Mary Kay and Tom for sharing their bat knowledge and anecdotes. Finally, to Linda for coming along and taking pictures during the bat observation trip (and sharing her bat rescue knowledge as well)—CW

Thanks to Laura Seckbach Finn, Director of www.FlyByNightInc.org: The Bat Specialists, for verifying the accuracy of the information in the book.

Publisher's Cataloging-In-Publication Data
Gerber, Carole.
Little red bat / by Carole Gerber ; illustrated by Christina Wald.

p. : col. ill. ; cm.

Summary: Takes young readers on an educational journey through one red bat's seasonal dilemma of hibernating or migrating. Includes "For Creative Minds" section.

Interest level: 4-8
Grade level: P-3
Lexile Level: 600, Lexile Code: AD
Also issued as auto-flip, auto-read, 3D-page-curling, and selectable English and Spanish text and audio eBooks
ISBN: 9781607180692 (hardcover)
ISBN: 9781607180807 (pbk.)

1. Bats--Juvenile literature. 2. Bats—Hibernation--Juvenile literature. 3. Bats--Migration--Juvenile literature. 4. Bats. 5. Bats--Hibernation. 6. Bats--Migration. I. Wald, Christina. II. Title.

QL706.2 .G47 2010
599.4   2009937786

Text Copyright 2010 © Carole Gerber
Illustration Copyright 2010 © Christina Wald
The "For Creative Minds" educational section may be copied by the owner for personal use or by educators using copies in classroom settings.

Manufactured in China, January, 2010
This product conforms to CPSIA 2008
First Printing

Sylvan Dell Publishing
976 Houston Northcutt Blvd., Suite 3
Mt. Pleasant, SC 29464